# THE ARCTIC

## BIOMES

Lynn M. Stone

The Rourke Corporation, Inc.
Vero Beach, Florida 32964

PHOTO CREDITS
All photos © Lynn M. Stone

**Library of Congress Cataloging-in-Publication Data**
Stone, Lynn M.
    The Arctic / by Lynn M. Stone.
       p.  cm. — (Biomes)
    Includes index.
    Summary: Explores the rugged and lonely wilderness of frozen
lands and icy seas which sweep around the top of the earth and
which are rich with wildlife and scenery.
    ISBN 0-86593-423-1
    1. Ecology—Arctic regions—Juvenile literature.  2. Arctic
regions—Juvenile literature.  [1. Ecology—Arctic regions.
2. Arctic regions.]  I. Title.  II. Series: Stone, Lynn M.  Biomes.
QH84.1.S763   1996
574.5'2621—dc20               95-46174
                                        CIP
                                        AC

Printed in the USA

# TABLE OF CONTENTS

# THE ARCTIC

Far north of North America's largest cities lies the Arctic region. It is a rugged and lonely wilderness of frozen lands and icy seas. It is also rich with wildlife and scenery.

The Arctic wraps around the top of the Earth, like a wide belt. Along with Greenland, the northernmost parts of Canada and Alaska make up North America's Arctic lands.

The highest Arctic lands are north of 65° **latitude** (LAT i tood) on a world map. Arctic animals and plants, however, begin to appear where the **tree line** (TREE LINE) ends.

*Mostly treeless, Arctic lands*
*wrap around the top of the Earth*

# ARCTIC TUNDRA

If you traveled north far enough, you would see the forests start to disappear. In their place, you would see **tundra** (TUN druh).

Tall trees cannot grow where the soil and weather conditions are too harsh. Where the tree line — the forest — ends, tundra begins.

Tundra is a soft, springy mat of low-lying plants — grasses, lichens, wildflowers, mosses, and dwarf trees. Tundra spreads like a great carpet across the Arctic.

*As trees disappear, far northern lands are covered by a carpet of tundra plants growing above the permafrost*

# LIFE ON THE TUNDRA

The tundra lies still and frozen in winter. Arctic temperatures in winter stay well below zero.

Spring brings a magical change — many hours of daylight and warm temperatures melt away snow. The tundra turns green. Great flocks of water birds arrive to lay eggs and raise young. The new plants become food for lemmings, hares, ground squirrels, musk ox, and herds of **caribou** (KARE uh boo).

The plant-eaters, in turn, feed Arctic foxes, wolves, snowy owls, falcons, and grizzly bears.

*The Arctic wolf hunts plant-eaters, such as mice, hares, and caribou*

# ARCTIC PLANTS

Each summer nearly all Arctic lands are free of snow and ice. A wild garden of over 1,700 **species** (SPEE sheez), or kinds, of Arctic plants blooms.

The plants support the Arctic's animal life on land. Without plants, the Arctic would be much like Antarctica.

Antarctica is the icy continent at the southern tip of the Earth. Very few plants grow on Antarctica. No land birds or mammals can live there.

*Arctic plants cushion a nesting golden plover — and support many kinds of northern animals*

*An all-year resident, the willow ptarmigan survives Arctic winters on the tundra by burrowing under the snow and eating twigs and berries*

*Born in June, the snow goose gosling will be grown up by late August and able to fly south with its parents*

# THE ARCTIC OCEAN

Tundra reaches to the shores of the Arctic Ocean. The icy Arctic Ocean is the smallest ocean in the world. Still, it's over 2,500 miles across at its widest point.

Next to the Antarctic, the Arctic Ocean is the world's coldest sea. It is covered with ice during much of the year.

Although cold, the Arctic Ocean is full of life. Shellfish, seals, whales, and fish feed on great swarms of **krill** (KRIL) and other sea creatures. Polar bears hunt seals on the ocean ice.

*The icy Arctic Ocean is
very rich in animal life*

## ARCTIC BIRDS

Each summer the cries of birds echo from rocky ocean islands and across the tundra. Noisy flocks of swans, cranes, and geese lead the bird chorus.

Snow geese and many other species feed on the tundra plants and insects. **Jaegers** (YAY gurz) and gulls rob the eggs of other birds. Snowy owls and falcons prey upon lemmings and other small animals.

Many songbirds — sparrows and their cousins — live among the tangles of grass and tiny plants.

*Hundreds of thousands of snow geese nest in the Canadian Arctic each summer*

## ARCTIC MAMMALS

Arctic hares, lemmings, voles, ground squirrels, and caribou keep busy nibbling on plants. Wolves, weasels, and foxes hunt birds and the plant-eating mammals.

The grizzly grazes on plants, gobbles up berries, and hunts animals, too.

Summer is a time of growth on the tundra, but winter makes changes in animal lives. Most caribou travel to the shelter of woodlands. The grizzlies and ground squirrels enter a long winter sleep called **hibernation** (hi ber NAY shun).

*Just one step ahead of winter, a grizzly hunts for berries on the autumn tundra*

# VISITING THE ARCTIC

The Arctic is far from the homes of most North Americans. Few roads reach the Arctic. Arctic travel is usually by plane, ship, or snowmobile.

Small groups of Native Americans live in Arctic villages. Visitors come to the Arctic to canoe, hike, hunt for gold, and study wildlife.

Visitors find autumn especially beautiful, but brief. In late August and early September, autumn paints the tundra leaves red, gold, and orange.

*September snow melts on autumn leaves of tundra blueberries and bear berries*

## PROTECTING THE ARCTIC

The Arctic is the last wild place of North America. Few people live there. However, oil, coal, and other valuable products are in the Arctic. More businesses and people will follow.

Meanwhile, Canada and the United States have set aside some Arctic lands to protect wildlife and the land. People can visit these **preserves** (pre ZERVZ), but they cannot develop them with roads, mines, and villages.

## Glossary

**caribou** (KARE uh boo) — a large, northern cousin of deer; wild reindeer

**hibernation** (hi ber NAY shun) — the deep, sleeplike state in which some animals survive the winter

**jaeger** (YAY gur) — a fierce, gull-sized bird of the Far North

**krill** (KRIL) — shrimplike animals of cold seas

**latitude** (LAT i tood) — imaginary lines that go around the Earth from east to west; latitude tells us how far north or south we are — the equator is at 0° latitude

**preserve** (pre ZERV) — a place set aside for the protection of its plants and animals

**species** (SPEE sheez) — within a group of closely-related plants or animals, one certain kind, such as a *polar* bear

**tree line** (TREE LINE) — the place at which forest trees can no longer grow because of harsh weather and soil conditions

**tundra** (TUN druh) — the "carpet" of low-lying plants that covers much of the ground in the Far North

# INDEX